Thank you for purchasing this cookbook!

Hopefully it will bring lots of color to your meals and keep you feeling healthy and energized.

The proceeds from your purchase will be added to an annual donation to Community Solidarity, an organization that provides groceries, fresh produce and warm vegan meals to low-income communities. Read more about their mission:
communitysolidarity.org

I've officially been a vegetarian since my college days but I've not always been a healthy eater. My vegetarian status was based on protecting animals more than nourishing myself. As a child I was a very picky eater and found many ways to avoid eating meat. In college, my roommate and I survived on raw carrots, popcorn, and coffee. Even into my 30's I didn't focus on nutrients or balanced meals and would often skip breakfast, eat a big cookie for lunch, and a bag of pita bread for dinner. I obviously didn't always have a healthy relationship with food.

I can honestly say that when my brother Nate and I launched *They Draw & Cook* (theydrawandcook.com) in 2010 my relationship with food began to shift. I became fascinated with food illustration and was inspired by the illustrated recipes that our wonderful community started sharing with us. I began paying attention to the mix of color and flavor in the meals I prepared. Most importantly, food became my friend, not my enemy.

In 2020, I became a vegan. It was an easy shift considering most of my non-vegan calories were coming from peanut M&M's and baked goods! It was definitely time to make the change.

For me the benefits of a plant-based diet have been remarkable. I enjoy preparing simple and colorful meals that don't require precise measuring or exact instructions. I find the chopping of veggies very calming and a nice transition from my workday into the evening hours.

This book gives a shout-out to Cleveland Kitchen (clevelandkitchen.com), an Ohio-based company dedicated to creating amazing fermented foods!

For old times sake, I still eat a bag of popcorn for dinner now and then.

Stay colorfully creative in the kitchen and on the drawing board!

SSSwindell

Salli S. Swindell

Many of these recipes can be easily changed-up based on the ingredients you have on hand and will lead you to create your own favorite variations!

EXTRA NOTES:

Drinking this first thing in the morning really sets you up for a fabulous day. A bit of fresh mint is also tasty.

GREEN SUNRISE
1 CUP CUBED RIPE PINEAPPLE
1 CUP FROZEN ORGANIC SPINACH
1/2 RIPE AVOCADO
JUICE OF 1/2 LIME
1 TSP FRESH GRATED GINGER
1 CUP COCONUT WATER
BLEND UNTIL SMOOTH
2 SERVINGS

EXTRA NOTES:

This is especially good during the warmer months. Omit the avocado if you want a thinner consistency.

Sunshine
GINGER CHIA
fresca
1 Blend 4 cups orange juice, 1 inch peeled & sliced ginger, 1/4 cup whole chia seeds until smooth
2 Strain
3 serve over ice with slice of lemon

EXTRA NOTES:

This is orange juice but better! Ginger is so good for your digestion and chia seeds are loaded with health benefits.

Minty
watermelon
juice

EXTRA NOTES:

No measurements needed for this. Add mint and lime according to your own taste. It's summer in a glass!

KIWI
THE WORLD'S HAPPY FRUIT
*it's BEEN proven THAT EATING 2 KIWI A DAY can ELEVATE YOUR MOOD & make YOU HAPPIER!
LITTLE RAYS OF SUNSHINE
you CAN EAT the SKIN TOO!

EXTRA NOTES:

I was amazed when I discovered all of the health benefits from one perfect little kiwi. I like eating them with bananas.

OH MY GOODNESS GRANOLA
What You NEED
1/4 CUP natural PEANUT BUTTER
1/4 CUP MAPLE SYRUP
3 TBS melted coconut OIL
1 tsp vanilla EXTRACT
1/4 CUP vegan chocolate CHIPS (mini)
2 1/2 CUPS ROLLED OATS
1/2 CUP SLIVERED ALMONDS
1/4 CUP unsweetened SHREDDED coconut
1/4 CUP COCOA POWDER
1/2 tsp Salt
what You DO
1 PReheat oven To 350°
2 whisk Together PB, vanill
maple SYRUP, coconut OIL
3 STIR in EVERYTHING ELSE EXCEPT chocolate CHIPS
4 SPRead on BAKING SHEET in even LAYER
5 BaKe 15-20 minutes (STIR HALFWAY THROUGH)
6 once COMPLETELY cooled, mix in CHOCOLATE CHIPS
SPRINKLE on Smoothie BOWL
or
CHIA PUDDING
or
Eat BY THE HandFUL

EXTRA NOTES:

Ok, so admittedly this granola tastes perfectly delicious without the chocolate chips but sometimes I just can't help myself.

RASPBERRY CHIA Jam
1. COOK 10.5 OZ. PACKAGE frozen RASPBERRIES & 4 TBS MAPLE SYRUP ON medium LOW FOR 10 min.
2. GENTLY SMASH BERRIES WITH FORK WHILE STILL IN PAN
3. ADD 1 TBS chia SEEDS & COOK 10 minutes more. COOL & ENJOY

EXTRA NOTES:

I was surprised that the chia seed really do soak up all the liquid! It's delicious on toast and oatmeal. Store in fridge.

EXTRA NOTES:

This is a great breakfast for those days when you'll be eating a late lunch. The nutty bits add extra crunch and vitamins.

2 1/2 CUPS Quickcooking OATS
1 CUP pumpkin SEEDS
1/8 TSP Salt
1/2 CUP DRIED CHERRIES
2/3 CUP ALMOND Butter
1/3 CUP mini CHOCOLATE CHips
1/2 CUP AGAVE
MIX OATS, SEEDS, Salt, CHERRIES And CHOCOLATE CHIPS in BOWL
Blend ALmond BUTTER And AGAVE To Smooth PASTE
STIR EVERYThing TOGETHER
PRESS MIX into Tinfoil Lined 8 X 8 PAN And COVER with PLASTIC wrap-PRESS Down AGain
place in FRIDge 4 HOURS
CUT into BARS {STORE in FRIDGE}
Peace & LOVE
NO-BAKE GRANOLA BARS

EXTRA NOTES:

You can use maple syrup in place of agave or different seeds and dried fruits. If it feels too dry add more agave.

TASTY TomaTOES on TOAST
• 2 CUPS CHERRY TOMatoes
• 2 CLoves GARLIC-minced
• 2 TBS OLive OIL, 2 TBS BALSAMic
BALSAMIC
SOURDOUgh BRead, Hummus, SunFLower SEEDS
• Mix OLive oIL, garlic and BALSamic with pinch of S+P ... TOSS with TOMAToes
• SPRead on BAKing TRAY and roast FOR 20 minutes at 375° until GOOEY!
• TOAST SOURDough and SPREad Layer of HUMMUS-ADD Tomatoes and SUNFLOWER seeds.

EXTRA NOTES:

I rarely use balsamic vinegar so I wasn't sure I would like this combination but it's one of my very faves! I could eat this for breakfast, lunch and dinner.

NUTTY SPICY Salad TOPPER
1/3 CUP sunFLower SEEDS
1 tsp. PAPRIKa
1 tsp. Cumin
salt + PEPPER
1/3 CUP PEPitas
1/2 CUP ALmonds
1 can CHICK PEAs (rinsed & DRiED)
Mix Everything TOGether & spread on BAKing SHEET
BAKE 25 min. 375°
sprinkle RED Pepper FLakes

EXTRA NOTES:

All I can say is that this mix tastes good on everything! I add it to salads, soups and roasted veggies. I love the spicy kick!

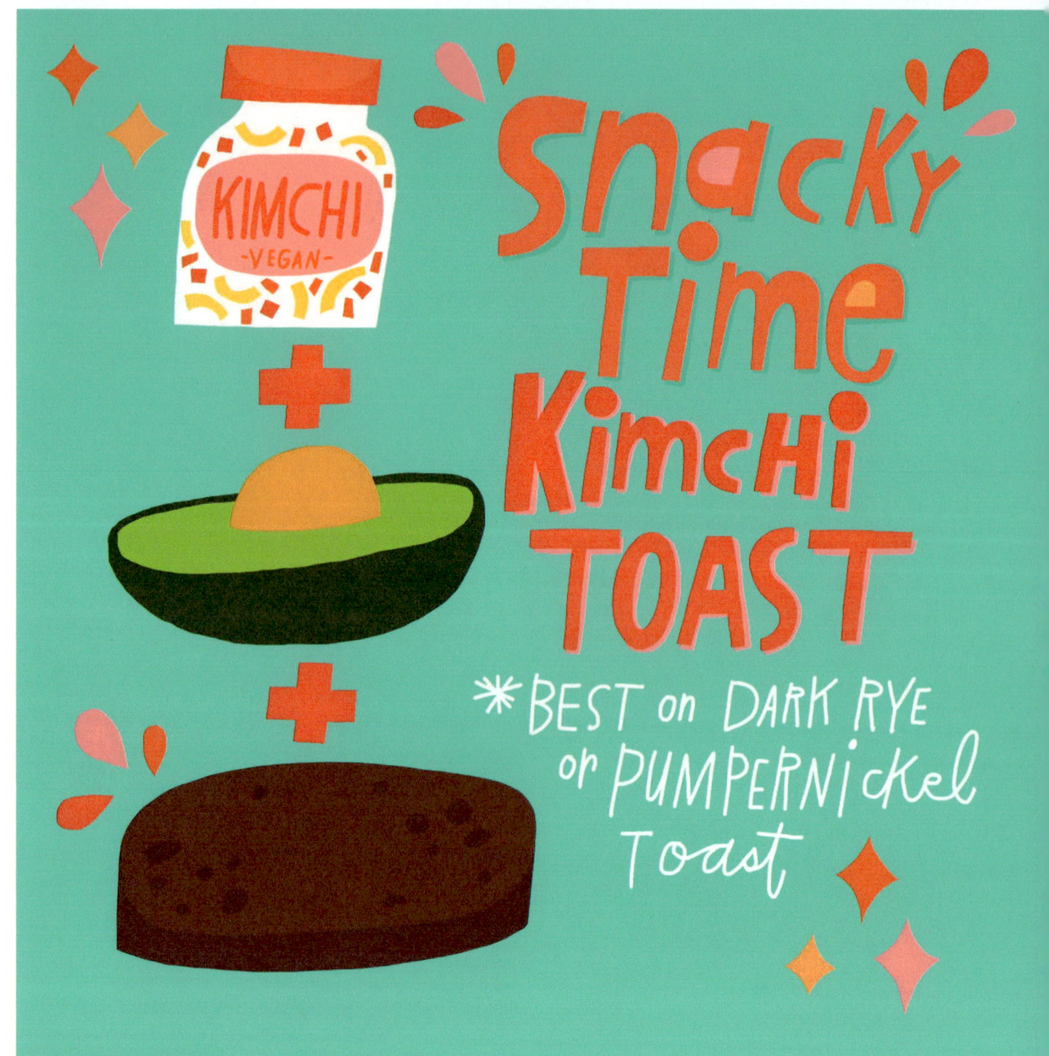
KIMCHI
-VEGAN-
Snacky Time Kimchi TOAST
*BEST on DARK RYE or PUMPERNickel Toast

EXTRA NOTES:

I never use to like kimchi but now I love it! This has happened with so many foods. As a kid I picked the onions out of everything, and now I eat them everyday.

EXTRA NOTES:

This is a delicious toast combination made even more scrumptious by a drizzle of Cleveland Kitchen Roasted Garlic Dressing!

HOT PINK Roasted Beet Hummus
BLEND TOGETHER:
•2 ROasted And PEELED BEEts
•1 CAn drained CHICK PEas
•1 TBS TAHini
•Juice OF 1 LEmon
•1 Garlic clove
•1 TBS OLive OIL
•S+P To Taste

EXTRA NOTES:

This hummus truly turns out to be hot pink and it's beautiful! I have the best success roasting fresh beets rather than using canned or packaged beets.

Roasted
RADISH
PREheat oven 425°
Cut off GReen Tops & SLice
RADishes in HALF – TOSS
with 1 TBS Avocado oil,
1/8 TSP GARLic POWDER,
Salt & PEPPER To Taste -
Roast 25 minutes
Sprinkle with fresh
PARSley & SQUEEZE of Lemon
LiTTLE RuBies

EXTRA NOTES:

I love a fresh peppery radish just as is but this is another option for enjoying the little gems. I've also used olive oil instead of avocado oil and might prefer it.

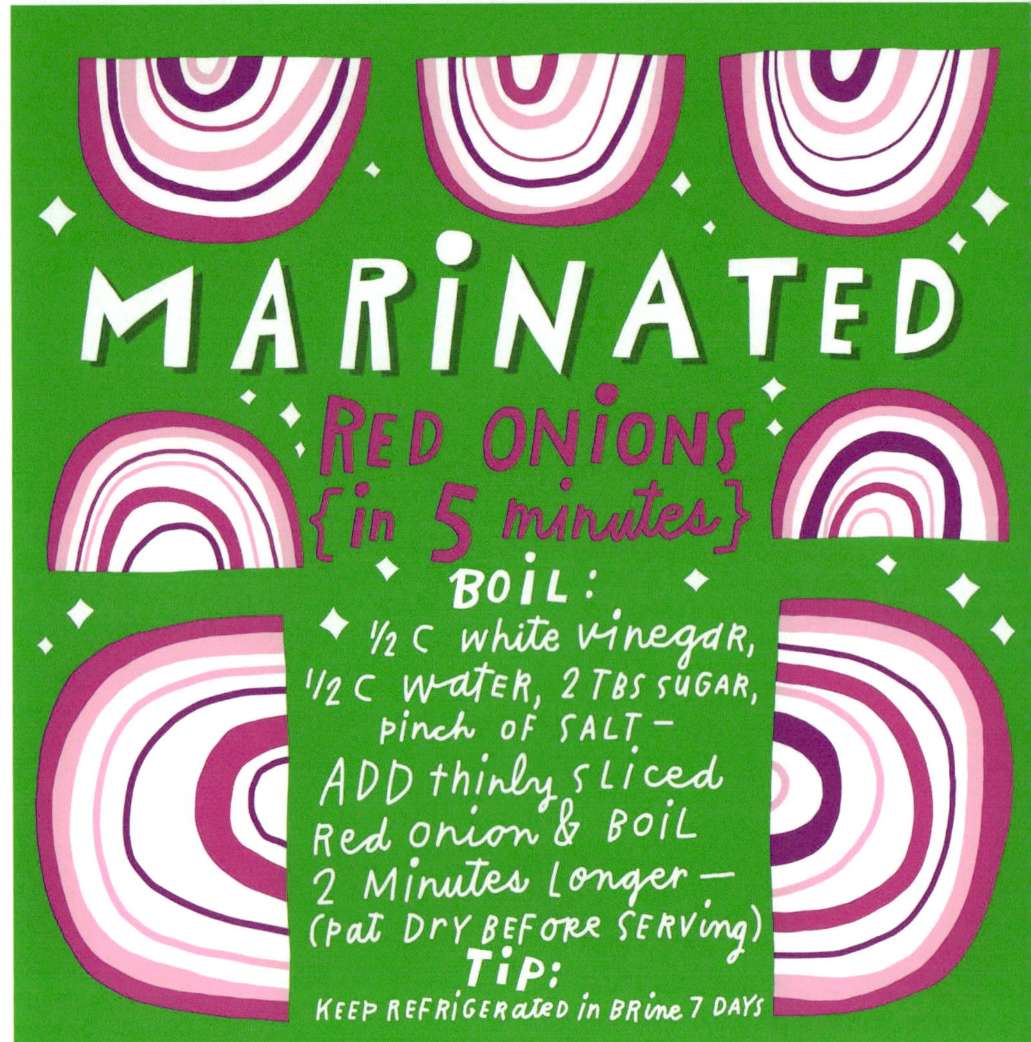
MARINATED
RED ONIONS
{in 5 minutes}
BOIL:
1/2 C white vinegar,
1/2 C water, 2 TBS sugar,
pinch of salt –
ADD thinly sliced
Red onion & BOIL
2 Minutes Longer –
(pat DRY BEFORE SERVING)
TIP:
KEEP REFRIGERATED in BRINE 7 DAYS

EXTRA NOTES:

For a recipe that takes such little time and effort, these red onions add BIG flavor. I think they taste great on vegan tacos, buddha bowls, and salads.

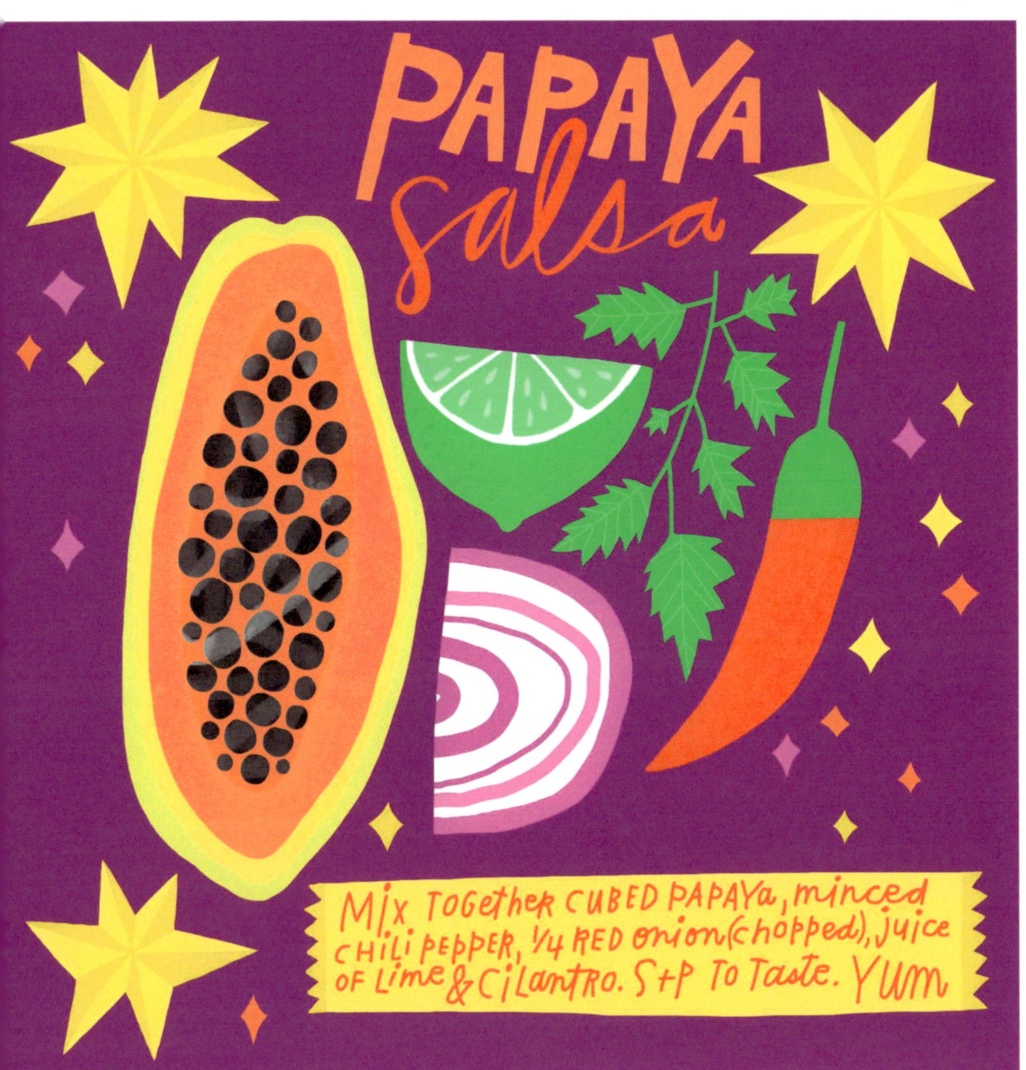
PAPAYA
salsa
Mix TOGether CUBED PAPAYa, minced CHILi PEPPER, 1/4 RED onion (chopped), juice OF Lime & CiLantRO. S+P TO Taste. YUM

EXTRA NOTES:

If you're not a fan of papaya try this with mango instead. A bit of pineapple might be nice also. Serve this super colorful salsa with blue corn chips.

ALL HAiL KALE
SUPER Tasty with AVOCado + ToasTed ALmonds
CUT AWay THICK STem & CHOP Leaves into Small PIECES
BEST DRESSinG!
• 1/4 CUP OLive OiL
• 3 TBS. TamaRi
• Juice oF one LEmon
• 2-3 TBS. TAHini
ADjust measURes PER Taste

EXTRA NOTES:

I never measure the ingredients for this dressing so it's a little different every time: zestier, creamier, saltier.

CLEVELAND
Kitchen
HAIL CAESAR
DRESSING & MARINADE
CREAMY & DAIRY FREE
PLANT-BASED
NATURALLY FERMENTED
NET WT. 12 FL OZ. (355ML)
Mmm ...mmm tasty
Hail Caesar
POTATO SALAD
2 LBS. RED POTATOES (CUBED + COOKED)
3 CARROTS SLICED
1 1/2 C. COOKED PEAS
4 RADISHES SLICED
4 SCALLIONS SLICED
1/4 PURPLE CABBAGE SLICED
TOSS WITH 1/4 C. OR MORE
CLEVELAND KITCHEN
HAIL CAESAR DRESSING

EXTRA NOTES:

This takes regular potato salad to the next level by adding tons more flavors like dijon mustard and caraway seed.

CRAZY
GREAT
CAULIFLOWER
• Preheat oven to 425°
• TOSS Cauliflower florets with
Olive oil, Generous sprinkle of
PAPRIKA, Cumin, Red pepper flakes, S+P.
• Arrange single layer on TRAY and
Roast 20-25 minutes.
• TOSS with salted pumpkin seeds.

EXTRA NOTES:

When I say this cauliflower is crazy great I really mean it! Adjust the spices to your taste preference. I often add this to my kale salad for a full meal.

Roasted CARROTS
12
carrots
cut in 2-inch
LENGTHS
4 TBS.
MAPLE SYrup
1/4 tsp.
cayenne
PEPPER
1 TBS. oLive oiL
1/4 tsp.
Each
SALT
PEPPER
minced CHives FOR garnish
PreHeat oven To 425°
→in ovenProof sKillet BRing oil, SYRUP, Cayenne and S+P To BoiL FOR 2 minutes. ADD CARROTS and Toss to coat.
→PLace CArrots in oven and cook 20 minutes. BRoiL for 2-3 minutes for extra char.
→REmove pan from oven and cook 2 more minutes on STOVETOP.
→SPRinkLe with minced CHives and serve!

EXTRA NOTES:

I've made this recipe with less maple syrup and the carrots are still just as tasty. Cooked carrots can be boring but not these!

NUTTY &NICE
PEANUT SAUCE
2 cloves garlic
1/4 CUP PEanut BUTTER
1/4 cup water
2 TBS Lime
1 tsp. Fresh grated Ginger
RICE VINEGAR
2 TBS each
TAMARI
Rice Vinegar
BLEND all TOGETHER
TOSS with SOBA noodles & Roasted Broccoli
SPRINKLE with crushed PEANuts

EXTRA NOTES:

This recipe comes with a warning label that you will want to eat it all the time! I often add more ginger and a jalapeño.

SUPER SAUCY
Delicious Tossed with Grains (FARRO, PASTA, Quinoa, Rice)
FOR a THinner SAuce ADD some VEG STOCK & Simmer
ADD Even MORE Vitamins BY Tossing in FRESH Spinach at End
HARISSA PASTE
CHOP 6 carrots, 1 Red PEPPER, 1/2 Onion into BiTe SIZE BiTS • Mince 2 cloves GARLIC • Halve 2 CUPS CHERRY TOMatoes • Rinse 1 CAN chick PEAS • Place EVERYthing in sKillet DRizzled with Olive oil • SEASON with S+P and 1/2 tsp. THYme • COOK on MEDium until VEGGIES SOFTEN Then STIR in 1 TBS. HARissa PASTE. SO YUM.

EXTRA NOTES:

Harissa paste! I had no idea how much I needed this ingredient until I finally tried it. This recipe is incredibly easy and so full of flavor and nutrients.

FABULOUS FENNEL SOUP
PRE·HEAT oven 350°
•TOSS FENNEL, onion, S+P and GARLIC with olive oil - arrange single layer on TRAY and Roast 20 min.
•BRING VEG stock to Boil - Add in Fennel mix and PEAS and Simmer 5 min.
•PURÉE - add coconut milk, lemon juice, spinach and parsley and Give one more quick puree
BIG HandFul Fresh Spinach
1/2 cup FROZEN PEAS
Splash Fresh Lemon
One Small onion, SLICED
2 GARLIC Cloves
1/2 c. coconut milk
3 CUPS VEG Stock
2 Fennel BULBS Trimmed & cut into THIN WEdges
BIG HANDFUL PARSLEY

EXTRA NOTES:

I'm the only one in my family that likes fennel so when I make this I know it will be my meal for days! Fennel loses a bit of its licorice tones when cooked this way.

GINGER
CARROT SOUP
8 carrots cut into 1 inch pieces
2 cloves GARLIC (minced)
2 inch CHUNK of Ginger (PEELed & minced)
1 jalapeño finely CHOPPed
1 can COCONUT MILK
1/2c - 1c VEG BROTH
2-3 CELERY STALKS (Diced)
OLIVE OIL
SAUTÉ veg in OLIVE OIL FOR 10 Minutes* add COCONUT MILK & SPLASH OF VEG BROTH* Simmer until carrots are SOFT* ADD more BROTH AS needed* Give a Quick PURÉE
SERVE with a dollop of CILANTRO PESTO, a SQUEEZE OF LIME and a SPRINKLE OF SALTED PEPITAS

EXTRA NOTES:

I like adding a HUGE amount of ginger to this recipe. If you like a thinner soup add more veg stock. I also serve with sourdough croutons. YUM.

VEGAN
WALNUT
TACO
CRUMBLE
(NO COOKING NEEDED!)
1 cup WALnuts
1 cup Mushrooms
1 TBS cumin
1/2 tsp GarLic POWDER
1/4 tsp Cayenne
Sprinkle S+P
1 TBS Tamari
Pulse Everything To a CRUMBLE (not a paste)

EXTRA NOTES:

Although this doesn't need to be cooked or heated, a quick skillet toss will soften up the ingredients and release the flavors of the spices.

THE BEST BUTTERBEANS
• 1 can DRAINED BUTTERBEANS
• 3 Roasted GARLIC CLOVES • HANDFUL PINE NUTS
• juice OF Lemon • HANDFUL FResh BASIL
• DASH OF WATER • 3/4 CUP FROZEN PEAS
• 2 HANDFULS FResh SPINACH
• PINCH OF SALT • 5 TBS OLIVE OIL
BLEND BASIL, GARLIC, PINE NUTS, LEMON, 3 TBS. OLIVE OIL SALT & WATER IN FOOD PROCESSOR UNTIL CHUNKY PESTO.
HEAT 2 TBS OLIVE OIL IN PAN - ADD BUTTERBEANS & COOK ABOUT 5 MINUTES UNTIL CRISP AROUND EDGES.
ADD PEAS, PESTO & SPINACH - COOK 5 TO 10 MORE MINUTES UNTIL SPINACH HAS WILTED. DELICIOUS!

EXTRA NOTES:

Don't be too worried if the beans break down a bit and become mushy. It still tastes really good! I like to toss it with leftover quinoa for added protein.

CREAMY Coconut RICE
STAUB
1 CUP Brown BASmati Rice
1 CUP coconut MILK
2 TBS grated coconut (SWEETened)
1/4 tsp. Salt
1 1/4 CUP water
1 tsp. Grated FResh Ginger
1 CLove gARLic crushed
3 TBS. fResh CiLantRo
Bring everything (minus CiLantRo) to Boil. Reduce Heat to Low & Simmer About 40-45 min. Remove From Heat
KEEP LID on For 10 more min. FLUFF with FORK, add CiLantRO
The KEY to PERFECT Rice is using a POT with a tight fitting LID

EXTRA NOTES:

I've tried many recipes for coconut rice and this is my favorite so far. It wasn't until I started using a pot with a very tight fitting lid that my rice cooked properly.

Hi-Five
ingredient
BEANS
SAUTé diced
Red onion &
minced GARLIC
Add 1 Can OF
GReat NorTHERN
Beans & Red CHILI
Flakes~
S+P.
TO
Taste
ADD fResh
SPinach,
Let WILT...
SQUEEZE of
Lemon JUICE

EXTRA NOTES:

Beans are a big source of protein and nutrients for me so having a stash of easy recipes on hand is essential. I definitely give these a high five!

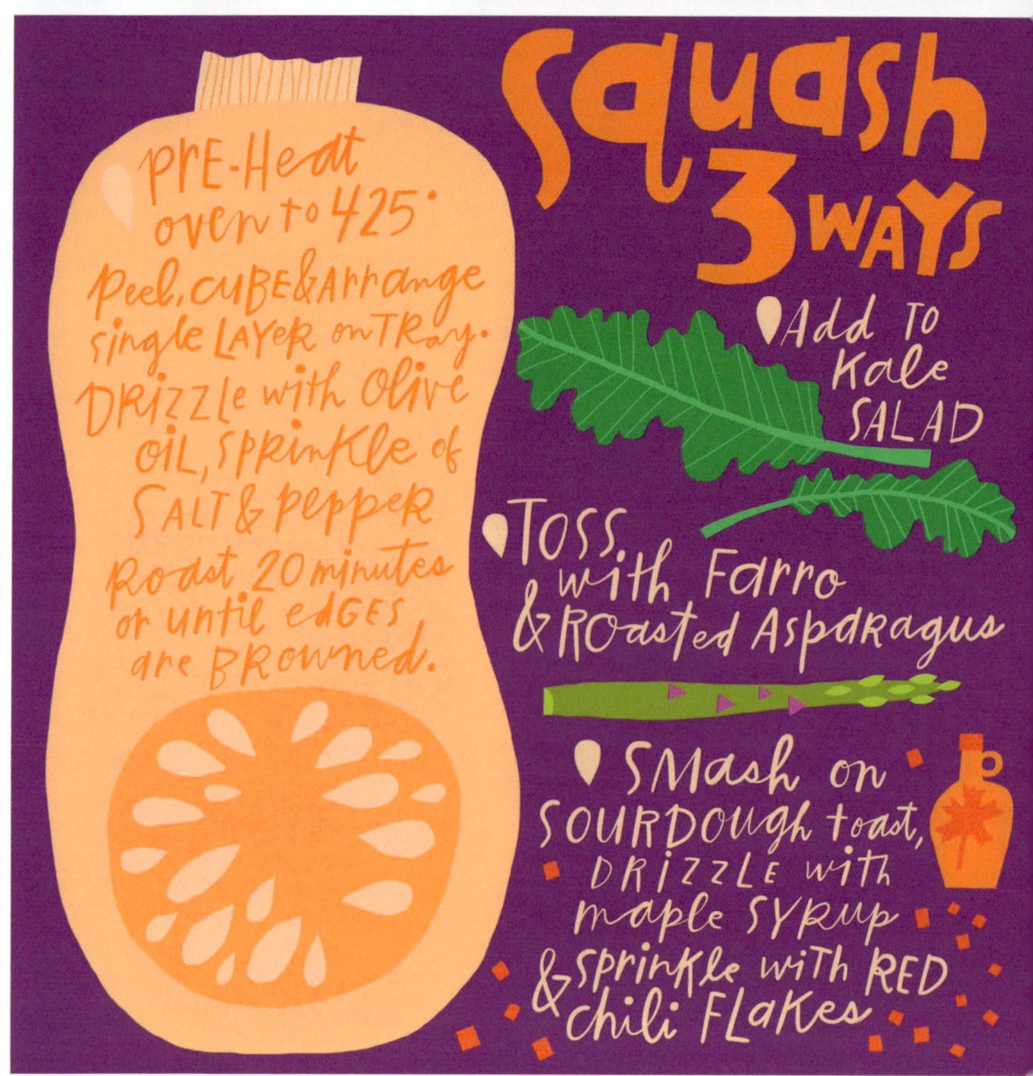
Squash 3 WAYS
PRE-Heat oven to 425°
Peel, CUBE & Arrange single LAYER on TRay.
DRIZZLE with Olive oil, SPRINKLE of SALT & PEPPER
Roast 20 minutes or until edGES are BROWNed.
Add To Kale SALAD
TOSS with Farro & ROasted Aspdragus
SMash on SOURDOugh toast, DRIZZLE with maple SYRUP & sprinkle with RED chili FLAKES

EXTRA NOTES:

Oh how I love squash! A drizzle of maple syrup to the toss adds a sweet caramelized flavor. I like roasting the squash until the edges are crispy.

EXTRA NOTES:

How gorgeous is this Sweet Beet Salad Dressing by Cleveland Kitchen? It's as yummy as its pretty pink color and tastes good on so many things.

PB caramel APPLes
6-8 APPLes
1/2 c. natural creamy PB
1/2 c. Brown Rice Syrup
3/4 c. chopped SALTED peanuts
• insert sticks
• cook PB + rice syrup over low heat until heated through - if too thick add more rice syrup
• spread mixture over apples with spoon
• sprinkle with nuts (press in place)
SET on tray lined with waxed paper + chill FOR 3 HOURS
* OPTional - TOASTED coconut
* PB = PEanut BUTTER!
* OPTional - MELTed VEgan CHOCOLate

EXTRA NOTES:

This is one recipe that looks better as an illustration! The real version isn't as smooth and glossy but they still taste amazing. The topping ideas are endless.

* Sunflower seeds are tasty too!
2 cups dried apricots
Apricot energy bites
1 cup pumpkin seeds
1 cup oats
Place everything in food processor & pulse until it forms a paste, leave some chunks in mix
1 cup desiccated coconut
2 TBS maple syrup
Great snack before & after workout
1/4 cup mini vegan chocolate chips
Shape into balls & place in fridge

EXTRA NOTES:

There is a ton of flavor in these little energy balls! They are also very filling. I always stir in the chocolate chips after I've mixed everything else together.

minty
Ginger
Tea
Steep several pieces of Ginger with mint leaves in Boiling water for several minutes... STRAIN & ADD Lemon slice

EXTRA NOTES:

I don't often drink tea but this really helps soothe a sore throat and warm up a cold winter night. I like using lots of ginger.

EXTRA NOTES:

Just a reminder to incorporate lots of these foods into your meals and try to eat at least 30 different plant-based ingredients every week!

Colorful Easy Vegan
by Salli S. Swindell
salliswindell.com

STUDIO SSS, LLC
Nate Padavick & Salli S. Swindell
studiosss.com

Made in the USA
Columbia, SC
05 June 2025

58947007R00024